THE BEAVER THAT LIVED IN THE TREES

James Kleist

The Beaver That Lived in Trees

This book is written to provide information and motivation to readers. Its purpose is not to render any type of psychological, legal, or professional advice of any kind. The content is the sole opinion and expression of the author, and not necessarily that of the publisher.

Copyright © 2020 by James Kleist.

All rights reserved. No part of this book may be reproduced, transmitted, or distributed in any form by any means, including, but not limited to, recording, photocopying, or taking screenshots of parts of the book, without prior written permission from the author or the publisher. Brief quotations for noncommercial purposes, such as book reviews, permitted by Fair Use of the U.S. Copyright Law, are allowed without written permissions, as long as such quotations do not cause damage to the book's commercial value. For permissions, write to the publisher, whose address is stated below.

Printed in the United States of America.

ISBN   978-1-951913-33-5   (Paperback)
ISBN   978-1-951913-34-2   (Digital)

Lettra Press books may be ordered through booksellers or by contacting:

Lettra Press LLC
30 N Gould St. Suite 4753
Sheridan, WY 82801, USA
1 303-586-1431 | info@lettrapress.com
www.lettrapress.com

Once upon a time there was a Daddy beaver, after he grew up he left his Momma and Daddy's home to make a home of his own and to have a big pond of his own.

This is where the fish and frogs could live and play and have fun all day long too. A place where the fish and frogs could have their families too. The deer, the elk, the moose and the bear all come there to drink water. Also the little critters like the squirrels, bunny rabbits, skunks, raccoons, badgers, coyotes and foxes, all have water to drink too. Soon the pond will have lily pads for the moose to eat as part of their diet.

So Daddy beaver was all grown up and in search of better place to make a beaver damn of his own. One day when he was swimming upstream, his eyes caught sight of a big beautiful Momma beaver. O' boy just what I need to help me build my damn to make my pond! And she has the oranges teeth I have ever seen, bet she could cut a tree down in a flash, he thought. Then Momma Beaver saw Daddy Beaver from a far-off and she thought, O great what a big ball of fur to keep me worm in the winter. Beaver fur is great for making felt hats known as 6X beaver, the more the Xs the higher the price of the hat will be. This is what the beaver trapper is after so he can make a living. Then the both of them thought; what a big tail you have to warn me of a dangerous predators. Beaver slap their tail on the water to warn the other beaver of the danger nearby. Then the beaver can hide in their hut; they can get in the hut from the pond because the door is in the bottom of the hut. The hut actually has two doors so they can go in one door and escape right out the other door. Even bears have hard time breaking in the hut.

So after getting to know each other for a while, the next day the construction of the damn began. So Daddy beaver and Momma beaver started to cut down trees to build their new home and damn. As they worked the damn got bigger and bigger and the hut stared to take shape. Soon the pond got deeper and deeper, and bigger and bigger. Soon afterward the little critters like bunny rabbits and squirrels and foxes and the deer came and also the elk and the moose came to drink water. After a time lily pads began to grow, then the moose had a staple food to eat in the summer time, in the winter time the moose eat willow twigs. Acetylsalicylic acid is one ingredient in willow and the American native would make a tea from willow to make a pain relief. Acetylsalicylic acid was the main active ingredient in aspirin.

After the lily pads began to grow in the pond then the frogs and the fish came to have families of their own and to swim and play and have fun all day long in the pond that Daddy and Momma beaver made. All the animals were having fun in the pond. Squirrels, the bunnies, foxes, deer and the elk and the moose were just enjoying themselves living by the pond. Lots of water and food was growing there. Then one spring day Momma beaver gave birth to a kit, a baby beaver.

Momma and Daddy beaver called him Bucky because Bucky had really big teeth bigger than normal. As Bucky grew up he learned how to climb trees. Beaver normally do not climb trees. Bucky was a great joy to all the other beaver in the pond, because when Bucky was a teenager he would climb to the tree tops and chew off all the small branches and send them down for all the other beaver to eat. The other beaver love him because they did not have to cut down any trees at all. There was food for all the other beaver to eat.

Now a year or two later when Bucky got much older, he decided to build a hut for himself. Not in a pond but in the tree tops high above the other animals. As he was branches off the trees, branches were flying everywhere to the right and to the left, just going everywhere. One day while Bucky was still building his hut in the treetops some big branches fell down on one of the elk's back. The elk when up to the moose to ask him what to do about Bucky and his hut in the tree. He said; "Today I was just grazing near his tree hut when a timber cracked and fell right on my back. What do you think we should do?" The moose didn't have no idea what to do. Then the deer came in on the conversation, the deer said; "I am going to just stay away."

Soon a squirrel came by and he squeaked out Bucky has so many branches chewed off, and I have no trees to climb up on.

So all the animals and the critters got together to figure out what to do to stop Bucky from tree waste. So they all walked the forest floor back and forth for many days wondering what to do.

Then one day Prickle a porcupine wondered into that part of the forest and he saw a beaver high up in a tree that had very few branches on it. Now Prickle was an old and wise porcupine. When Prickle got to the tree where Bucky was in, he waddled over to climb up to Bucky. Then Prickle asked Bucky why are you living up here in the tree tops? Don't you think you should be living in a pond that you built? How is a mate going to come up here when beaver normally do not climb up trees?

Then Bucky began to think about what Prickle said. Then Bucky started to remember what his Mom and Dad did they built a damn and had a pace to swim and store food to eat even in winter. Plus all the other animals are very happy and having fun all day. After a day or two Prickle came back to Bucky's lodge and asked Bucky, "Did you ever see how your lodge is bending down the tree branches? On top of that it is about to break and down it will come." He drew the conclusion that he could not have a mate up there either. Then Prickle said "Even if your mate could come up here and that branch brook off you and your mate would have no place to live." Finally Bucky got the point. "Great wood chips." Bucky thought to himself. "I never thought of that as consequences to the other animals and small critters like the squirrels, bunnies and such could get killed!

Then Prickle said to Bucky, "Let me help you take apart your tree lodge and I'll show you a great place to build a great beaver damn and lodge upstream from your Mom and Dad's pond. So come on with me to my lodge where there is plenty of water in the creak." When they got to Prickle's lodging place, Bucky said "O wow! This place is really great! I think it is fantastic it is even better then Mom and Dad's place. The land has a great valley with lots of trees. Look at all the aspen trees! O wow yummy. Hey over there are some birch trees too."

Then Prickle said and my lodging place is just over there in that spruce tree on the hill. Then Bucky thanked Prickle for helping him find the great place to build a beaver damn and Prickle said you are welcome. And thought to himself now I don't have to walk so far to get water to drink and I'll have deer, elk and moose antlers to chew on when I need calcium for my diet. Porcupines have orange teeth too and the keep growing just the same as the beaver.

In the winter the deer, elk and the moose shed their antlers and grow a new set of antlers that are bigger than the year before.

As Bucky was walking over to size up one of the birch trees to cut it down, to get started on his dam, why look over there; O' wow, a girl beaver Bucky's same age coming to build a dam for herself. So Bucky stopped cutting down the tree he just began chewing on, and went over to introduce himself to the girl beaver and to get acquainted with her.

After all she would help build the dam he planned and keep each other worm in the winter and start a family. So Bucky went up to the girl beaver to ask her, her name, but she just ran a way and so Bucky ran after her and around and around they chased each other. This went on for about 3 or 4 hours. Then she said my name is Buffy, what is yours? Then Bucky said; Hi Buffy my name is Bucky. Then around and around they chased each other until they were completely tired out.

Then Bucky and Buffy got up early in the morning and finished cutting the tree down that Bucky started the day before. Before they knew it the dam was built and the hut was well on the way. After two or three weeks the hut was finished.

And now Bucky and Buffy could swim and play all day and the deer, elk, the moose, the bears the little critters like the foxes and squirrels and the bunny rabbits all had food to eat and water to drink, thanks for Bucky and Buffy's dam. Soon fish and frogs were swimming in the pond and having fun all day. After a year then Bucky and Buffy started a family and lived happily ever after and having fun all day long.

The morel of the story is be nice to others no matter what color they are and there will be a reward for you in the future.

www.ingramcontent.com/pod-product-compliance
Lightning Source LLC
Chambersburg PA
CBHW081800100526
44592CB00015B/2506